WILL

A Memoir

of

"The Father of British Geology"

(1842)

Edited by

Peter R. Jenkins

Dragonwheel Books

1996

Printed and Published by Dragonwheel Books 1996
Sandcott   Rectory Lane,
Pulborough,
West Sussex,
RH20 2AD

Memoir first published 1842
This edition with notes Copyright © Dragonwheel Books 1996

British Library C.I.P. Data:
A Catalogue Record is available from the British Library

ISBN   1 870177 25 8

William Smith - A Memoir

For the advance of most sciences two kinds of men are necessary - first, the active observing man who bustles about collecting facts, then the meditative reflecting man who systematises those facts and draws conclusions. Geology is eminently one of the sciences requiring two classes of cultivators. The first was more particularly necessary forty or fifty years ago, when the science only existed in its rudest elements. At that time there were two widely different men engaged in investigating the aqueous rocks - the German mine superintendent Werner,[1] a sublime genius, who theorised before he had largely enough observed, and William Smith, an English land surveyor, who only could observe. To the latter, mainly the world has been indebted for its knowledge of the order in which that class of rocks has been formed above each other. Mr Smith is only the more remarkable for this service, from his being purely a practical man, one who had few opportunities for study and no theory to lead him on and reward him for his labours. His attendance at meetings of the British Association was well remembered by those present, but even when possessing name and fame, he looked only like a rather homely kind of farmer.

In order that his work may be appreciated by a wider public, the following memoir is furnished by one who knew him.

*   *   *

William Smith was born, March 23rd, 1769, at Churchill, Oxfordshire - over, as he was fond to remark, the oolitic formation. He commenced as a geologist in his very boyhood, it being one of his earliest amusements to collect the fossil shells which abound in this class of rocks, and to observe their several characters. His patrimony being small, he engaged in the profession of a surveyor of land; and in the course of acquisition of professional knowledge, it was his delight to store facts in reference to the strata whose surfaces he measured and apportioned as a matter of business. In 1791, Mr Smith was employed in Somersetshire; and some years later he was engaged in executing the Somerset Coal Canal.

Here he frequently descended the coal pits, and obtained much information on the coal measures from the colliers and his own keen personal inspection. In the course of this period, he became intimately acquainted with the minute characteristics of the stratification around Bath, which including the coal measures, embraced some of the most important of our English rocks and clays. He in time collected numerous organic remains, all of which he was careful to label in reference to the precise positions from which they were derived. He was now called to survey on the Cotswold Hills; and, early in 1794, to attend Parliament in connexion with the business of the Somerset Coal Canal Company. His journey to London, afforded him an opportunity, thoroughly made use of, of observing the contours of the hills and eminences in the various neighbourhoods; nor was the conformation of ranges of knolls and minor elevations lost upon our observer   A stagecoach journey was in fact to him the perusal, though necessarily a hasty perusal, of a page of nature's volume. He was wont to relate with particular zest the history of a long, but to him by no means tedious, travel which he undertook with two engineers, in 1794, to the north of England, for the purpose of collecting information on canals and collieries. Seated foremost in the chaise, he explored every point of broken ground on two lines between Bath and Newcastle-on-Tyne; and, instructed by previous observations, he correctly interpreted the hieroglyphics presented by the contours of distant hills, and traced, by aid of these and the form and position of escarpments, the strata of Bath to the coast of Whitby, and the chalk of the Wiltshire downs to the wolds of Lincolnshire and Yorkshire.

At this period of his life, Mr Smith was entirely unacquanited with books on the physical geography and natural history; although, even if he had been learned in their lore, there was little at that time published that could have materially assisted him in his inquiries. His ignorance was proved by numerous particulars; and chiefly by his adoption of the local designations of the particular strata, and the employment of such terms as would be recognised in the respective neighbourhood of the rocks. Many of these, however inharmonious - such as combrash, forest marble, lias - are still preserved in the alphabet of geology, while others have yielded to more correct denominations.

In 1795, when Mr Smith became a householder, he began to arrange his collections of fossils from the vicinity of Bath, *in the order of the strata;* and before 1799 he had coloured geologically the large sheets of the Somersetshire survey, and a circular map of the vicinity of Bath, both remarkably accurate.

By maps and sections, also, he explained to numerous scientific gentlemen, who were attracted by the novelty of his system to visit him, those views relating to the regular succession and continuity of strata, and the definite distribution of animal and vegetable remains in the earth, which are now placed in the first lessons of geology. The great distinctive features of Mr Smith's system were now clearly presented to his own mind and to the minds of others. They were these: - That the fossil productions of the several strata are not accidentally and confusedly distributed in them, but that each species has its own peculiar place as belonging to some particular stratum; that this species may be either confined to that stratum only, or to that and other particular strata in conjunction; that in the first case it becomes an infallible test of the identity of two strata occurring in two different localities, and in the last case a collateral proof of that identity.

Mr Smith arranged (for convenience of removal) the fossils in trays, letting down one above the other, in boxes of moderate dimensions; each box commonly containing a collection of fossils from the same rock or stratum in various parts of England. As they were nearly all collected by his own hands, he could point with certainty to the proofs of his theory of identification of strata by organic remains; and the theory was therefore fully established, and gradually made known and received. In all these exhibitions and explanations, we are especially called upon to admire the liberality and frankness of his communications to any respectable and intelligent inquirer. He reserved no portion of information to himself, but profusely bestowed it without considerations of selfishness, or thought of compensation of any kind. Had he been actuated by any thing apart from an indomitable love of the science, it is no more than probable that his knowledge might have been turned to good account for his own exclusive benefit in his profession. On the contrary, it was perpetually evident that he made his profession subservient to his pursuit of geology. His devotion to the science was evidenced by his receiving about this time a designation by which he was usually distinguished throughout his life from the innumerable multitude of Smiths who inhabit our island - namely, that of "Strata Smith".

Dr James Anderson[2] and other scientific gentlemen urged Mr Smith to lay his views and discoveries before the world, and offered him such assistance as was in their power, which offers were repeated on the part of other men of eminence.

In 1799, therefore, appeared a small *Tabular Views of the Superposition of English Strata*; and in 1801, a prospectus for an *Accurate Delineation and Description of the Natural Order of the Various Strata of England and Wales*. This prospectus is in itself a brief compendium of the practical applications of geology, and displays the growing mastery of the subject, which was finally proved beyond a doubt by the appearance, in 1815, of the principal portion of his *Delineation of the Strata of England and Wales*. This work was a large map, in fifteen coloured sheets, of the kind now known as geological maps, and was the unaided production of this one zealous geologist. Considered in this light, and also, indeed, of a near approach to general accuracy, its merits can scarcely be overrated. Although it was not long after followed by the more accurate map of Mr Greenough,[3] it is not difficult to suppose that the formation of the latter was facilitated by the labours of Mr Smith, at least in diffusing geological knowledge over a large portion of England. Nor must it be forgotten that he had long prepared the main parts of his map, but did not meet with sufficient encouragement to publish it. Sir Joseph Banks had become acquainted with our geologist in one of his visits to the agricultural meetings, called "sheep-shearings", at Woburn and Holkham, and afterwards proved a warm patron and the promoter of a subscription to assist the publications of our author.

In 1804 Mr Smith had removed to London, and in 1806 he published a treatise on irrigation. From this period up to 1815, he had attracted notice in various ways; and in that year, when his great map appeared, the British Museum purchased his whole collection of fossils for £500. The task of arranging these led to the publication of two small quartos, entitled *Strata Identified by Organised Fossils* (1815); and *Stratigraphical System of Organised Fossils* (1817), the latter being designed as an index to the specimens in the museum. Between the appearance of the great map in 1815 and 1821, Mr Smith published no less than twenty geological maps of English counties, often remarkable for their near approach to accuracy. It is, however, painful to record the fact, that all his efforts have been insufficient to ensure himself a moderate or even small (financial) competency. He was compelled to forego his residence in London, and in some degree to lead a wandering life in various parts of the country. In 1824 he delivered a course of lectures to the members of the Yorkshire Philosophical Society, and repeated these the same year, in conjunction with his nephew (the well-known Professor Phillips, the author of several works on geological subjects), at Scarborough and Hull.[4]

In 1825 similar lectures were delivered at Sheffield, and efforts were made to secure some permanent engagement for Mr Smith. He at length was offered and accepted an occupation as agent to Sir John Johnstone, Bart.,[5] at the beautiful retreat of Hackness, near Scarborough. Here, as usual, he set himself to geological research, the result of which soon appeared in a map and a collection of fossils. I shall ever remember the hearty shake of a weathered hand with which he welcomed me to Hackness, whither I had repaired to reside with him for some time as a pupil. He, on this occasion, set myself and a friend who accompanied me down to a bread and cheese luncheon; but before our hunger was half appeased, he insisted on hauling us out to inspect the outline of the neighbouring hills. My friend, who professed no passion for practical geology, could not leave the cottage without casting at least "one long, lingering look behind".

Mr Smith subsequently spent the main portion of his time at Scarborough, the vicinity of which is rich in objects of geological interest. He had, as early as 1817, planned the arrangements of the beautiful museum at that place, and it was erected and carried out upon his plan. The building is circular, and the fossils and the geological and mineralogical contents are arranged in sloping shelves, one above the other, in such a manner that the circle presents a good silent lecture on the strata. The order of natural superposition is followed, and thus the positions and productions of the several strata are at once observed.[6]

The practical value of his knowledge has been most triumphantly proved in the instance of the Great South Hetton Colliery in Durham. For, in 1821, Mr Smith recommended to Colonel Braddyl, the proprietor of the estate, to search for coal *beneath* the magnesian limestone. The idea of such a search was always previously held to be one of very great uncertainty in its result, and by some was entirely scouted. The issue of the experiment has proved the most fortunate possible for Colonel Braddyl and others; for excellent coal has been obtained, although not without considerable difficulties in sinking the shafts.

Our geologist was intensely gratified, and partially rewarded for comparative obscurity, in the presentation to him, in 1831, by the Geological Society of London, of the first Wollaston medal, accompanied by a merited and eloquent eulogium by Professor Sedgewick, in the course of which he styled Mr Smith the "Father of British Geology".[7] The British Association, assembled at York that year, made application to government for a pension to Mr Smith, which was ultimately settled upon him for life, to the amount of £100 annually.

The crowning gratification of our philosopher was bestowed at Dublin, in 1835, when the University, during the meeting of the British Association in that city, conferred upon him the degree of LLD. On the first day of the meeting of the Association I encountered him, as I was hurrying to the assembly, in the street, and, ignorant of his new honour, cordially addressed him in the usual style of Mr Smith, which designation he instantly paused to assure me was defunct, and dilated with pardonable vanity upon his doctorship. Occasionally, on passing him during the day, I overheard him explaining to other friends the error into which their ignorance, like mine, had led them; and even on the last day of the meetings of the Association, the same verbal correction was being administered to the last ignorant delinquent.

Several of his friends expected the pleasure of again conversing with him, in 1839, at the meeting of the British Association in Birmingham. Great, however, was our regret and surprise to hear, upon our arrival there, that Dr Smith had closed his life and labours at Northampton, September 23rd, while on a visit to a friend, in his way to the meeting. It was a remarkable coincidence, that a wish of his, often half-jocularly expressed, had been realised in the site of the place of his death. He had often said that he wished he might close his labours on the stratum on which he had commenced them - namely, the oolite. Northampton is situated on the oolite! And in St. Peter's churchyard repose, on that very stratum, the remains of "Strata Smith".

I have enumerated the titles of the principal publications of Dr Smith; but with the exception of the great map and the other maps, they were usually but partially complete, and were obviously intended more as preludes to sustained efforts to be made under more favourable circumstances. This admission does not detract from his justly earned fame, but it will account for the fact that their author has been almost forgotten, except among his immediate circle of friends. He was in the habit also, during many of his latter years, of recording his recollections and ideas based upon them, upon separate slips of paper, in a neat handwriting. These slips accumulated to a formidable extent - so formidable, indeed, as to render the chance of their arrangement and reperusal very remote. He one day opened all these stores to me, and urged upon me the desirableness of reducing them to order and methodical arrangement. I undertook the task with some perseverance and ardour; but ultimately relinquished it, from the utter impossibility of accomplishing the project satisfactorily - as indeed, such a loose mode of composition might naturally have led me to anticipate.

It must not be concealed, however, that Dr Smith's views were not exactly accordant with the advanced state of geological science in his latter years. He could by no means be brought to acquiesce in the theories propounded by some of our bold modern investigators; nor was he always sparing in his attempts to disprove or disparage them, whether justly or not it is not my purpose here to determine. But I well remember with what an indignant zest he was occasionally wont to exclaim against the fashionable tendency to refer particular distortions or depositions to particular and secondary agency; and the modern readiness to create a special cause for every special event and effect. These dissertations he used generally to conclude by saying - "Ah! sir, these modern theorists only want to make out the Creator *a journeyman!*" Such pithy apothegms were frequently, for example, introduced in his discussions with me upon the vegetable origin of coal - a theory in which he was by no means disposed to acquiesce.

His brother geologists always very properly paid a due degree of respect to the venerable founder of their improved and certain system of observation; and hence seldom controverted his opinions so ardently as they might otherwise have been disposed to do. Hence too, it was by common and ready consent that an honourable seat, amongst the chief men of the section, was always assigned to "Father Smith" at the meetings of the British Association. These meetings were, indeed, his glory and comfort in his declining days, and were looked forward to by him with a degree of intense interest that ordinary people could not understand or appreciate.

I was present with him at every meeting of the Association except the two first; and was always much delighted with the paternal interest with which he appeared to regard the proceedings of his sons, if they might be called - which is the more questionable, perhaps, as he considered some of them very far from dutiful in their unruly attempts at theorising. While we were one morning breakfasting with Professor Sedgwick, at the Cambridge meeting of the Association, a very good-humoured paternal correction was gently administered to the accomplished professor, and most dutifully received by him, although it does not appear by his subsequent course that it was productive of serious effects upon him.

Latterly, Dr Smith was afflicted with deafness to some extent; but this did not prevent his attendance at the several meetings of the Association, and his occupation of a doctor's chair in all seeming state.

Occasionally the lecturer for the day would turn aside towards him, and utter in a louder key some complimentary allusion to the "father of English geology"; whereupon it was most delightful and amusing to witness the conscious merit of the venerable philosopher, and the warm respect of the *illuminati* around him. These allusions, deaf as he was, he never failed to hear and treasure up, to be retailed on all fitting occasions to those who had not the privilege of hearing them at their birth. But especially after his reception of the Wollaston medal, I imagine, no stranger was introduced to Dr Smith without at the same time being introduced by him to the medal. The old man carried it about with him in its red leather case wherever he went, and was ever able to lay his hand upon it at a moment's warning. Before the form of the introduction of any stranger was well nigh completed in all its ceremonies, the doctor's hand was in his pocket, and in an instant he would commence in a kind of low utterance, "This is my medal", etc. Some of us were scarcely able to restrain a smile upon such occasions.

Nor, if any stranger was present at breakfast with him, were we unacquainted with what would prove the theme of conversation; and usually we so far gratified him as to prevail upon the servant to arrange things in a convenient manner; for, upon the first break of the uniformity of the plate of bread and butter, the doctor would turn with a complacent semi-smile to the stranger and say - "Now, that plate of bread and butter occurs to me as a capital exemplification of the order of the strata. You see, they crop out and overlie each other, just as the pieces of bread do. There, you see, you may form a good notion of the oolite beds by that arrangement. Suppose that we double these pieces, thus, we represent a distortion," etc.

It will readily be conceived from these remarks that Dr Smith was an acute observer of common, and hitherto usually neglected, facts. To the last walk of his life, he geologised as he walked; and from the first days of his life he thereby acquired an invincible habit of looking on the ground if walking, and on the fields if riding. A spring in a field, a stone, a building, a quarry, a clay-pit, brick-field, lime-kiln, and even a ploughed field, were all made to administer to his favourite science, and all to minister well, though not always with novelty. By this perpetual observance of the qualities and properties of external objects, continued throughout an active life, he became not only an interesting companion to the unoccupied stroller, but a profitable fellow-traveller to the practical man.

Hence he was appointed to accompany Mr Barry and other commissioners upon their investigations into the durability and suitableness of the stone for the new Houses of Parliament; and he frequently astonished these gentlemen by the accuracy of his local knowledge, and the variety of his predictions as to the course and quality of certain rocks. No opportunity of studying the properties of stone was neglected by him, and no time was deemed unsuitable by him for such inquiries. If attending a parish church to which he was a stranger, he was sure to spend some time in the churchyard, observing how far the stones had become worn by the weather in proportion to their age. I have more than once walked with him through such a scene, while he pointed out the stratum and locality from which every tombstone was derived.

My friend (above alluded to) who accompanied me to Hackness, was a zealous and most pious clergyman, and, as was his wont, immediately commenced a professional crusade against the man of science, in which, after numerous assaults, he had to confess himself foiled - not by the opposition of the philosopher, but by his perfectly quiet acquiescence in all he propounded, and his reception of the applied force without a particle of reaction, save that every remark of the professional man was dexterously directed by the philosopher to the advanced state of geology. My pious friend raised the siege upon being most thoroughly deceived by the meditative appearance of Dr Smith on one occasion in Scarborough churchyard. The doctor was poring pensively over the tombstones, and thereby deluded my friend into the belief that his opportunity for instilling his advice was indubitably arrived - a conclusion which he discovered to be hopelessly fallacious, when the real nature of the doctor's cogitations was made known.

Dr Smith's moral conduct and character were most exemplary throughout his whole life; and his unfailing kindness in circumstances of the most trying domestic affliction, were no less conspicuous and praiseworthy than his unshaken fortitude in bearing up against pecuniary difficulties. It was remarkable that his cheerfulness and hilarity continued almost to the last day of his life. He died indeed of natural decay, at the age of seventy-one, and without pain; his temperate and active habit, together with the healthy character of his pursuits, having kept him hale to the last.

*　　*　　*

NOTES

1 Abraham Gottlob Werner, (1750-1817) - Born in Silesia, he explored rock formations in the mines of the Hartz mountains and in 1774 published a study of mineralogy. Soon after, he was appointed to lecture on geology and mining at Freiburg, Saxony. Seeking to apply his theories to the whole of the Earth's crust, he maintained what became known as the 'Neptunian theory', that all rocks were deposited by sedimentation in water, and discounted a volcanic origin for igneous rocks. His lectures were reported and published, and in 1791 appeared his *New Theory on the Formation of Metallic Veins*, which was translated into French and English. In 1792 he was nominated counsellor of the mines in Saxony, a post which included administration of public works.

2 Dr James Anderson, (1739-1808) - Born at Hermiston, near Edinburgh, by the age of fifteeen Anderson was managing farms there and in Aberdeenshire. He wrote many works on both agriculture and political economy, and was granted a doctorate by the University of Abedeen in 1780. He was commissioned by the government to make a survey of fisheries in 1784, and retired to Isleworth in 1797.

3 George Bellas Greenough, F.R.S., (1778-1855) - Educated at Eton and Pembroke College, Cambridge, and Gottingen and Freiburg. M.P. for Gatton, 1807-12. First President of the Geological Society, 1811-13, also 1818 and 1838. President of the Royal Geographical Society, 1839-40. Published a *Critical Examination of the first Principles of Geology* (1819) and geological maps of Great Britain (1820).

4 John Phillips F.R.S., (1800-1874) - Nephew of William Smith. Secretary of the Yorkshire Philosophical Society and Keeper of the York Museum 1825-40. One of the founding members of the British Association, and its Assistant Secretary, 1832-59. Professor of Geology, Trinity College, Dublin 1844-53. Keeper of the Ashmolean and University Museums, 1854-74. Professor of Geology at Oxford, 1856-74. President of the Geological Society, 1859-60.

    The first meeting of the British Association was held in York in 1831, due indirectly to William Smith's lectures.

The Yorkshire Philohsophical Society had been formed in the city in 1822 by four local men, one of whom, the Reverend William Vernon, was the son of Edward Vernon, then Archbishop of York. One of the prime aims of the Society was the study of Yorkshire's geology, and it was Vernon who arranged for William Buckland to visit Kirkdale Cave to investigate the prehistoric animals bones found there. In 1824 it was also Vernon who invited William Smith to lecture to the members of the Society, but 'although Smith's discourses were successful enough, it was (John) Phillips, his young nephew and assistant, who impressed by his energy, his eloquence and his varied scientific talents. At the beginning of 1826 he was officially designated keeper of the Museum of the Yorkshire Philosophical Society, at a salary of £60 per annum.'* By the spring of 1829 this energy, directed into a combination of field-work and study of the Society's specimens, enabled him to publish the first part of his *Illustrations of the Geology of Yorkshire*, which was dedicated to William Smith.

In February 1831 David Brewster, the Scottish scientist and inventor of the kaleidoscope, proposed the establishment of 'a Society of British Cultivators of Science', and when he wrote to John Phillips to ask if the Society would help, both he and William Vernon were enthusiastic. Support was found from the City corporation and others, and on 12 July the Yorkshire Philosophical Society issued a public circular to other societies and individual 'cultivators and promoters of science'.*

Vernon, who had taken in addition the name of Harcourt on his father inheriting the family estates that year, chaired a committee of management, and on Monday 26 September 1831 a first meeting was held of what would become the British Association. Appropriately, John Phillips gave the first scientific address, on the subject of the geological features of Yorkshire. He served as asssistant secretary to the Association until 1862, and presided at the Birmingham meeting in 1865. William Vernon Harcourt was appointed general secretary and served until 1837; he was president in 1839, also at a Birmingham meeting, in the year of William Smith's death.

* 'Science in early nineteenth-century York: the Yorkshire Philosophical Society and the British Association' by Derek Orange, an article published in *York 1831-1981, 150 Years of Scientific Endeavour and Social Change*, ed. C.H. Feinstein (York, 1981).

Meeting	President
1831 - York	Viscount Milton
1832 - Oxford	Rev. William Buckland
1833 - Cambridge	Rev. Adam Sedgwick
1834 - Edinburgh	Sir Thomas Makdougall Brisbane
1835 - Dublin	Rev. Bartholomew Lloyd
1836 - Bristol	The Marquis of Lansdowne
1837 - Liverpool	The Earl of Burlington
1838 - Newcastle-upon-Tyne	The Duke of Northumberland
1839 - Birmingham	Rev. William Vernon Harcourt

5 Sir John Vanden Bempde Johnstone, Bart., DCL., the second Baronet, was born at Hackness Hall in 1799, son of Sir Richard Johnstone, who had purchased the manor three years before. Sir John succeeded to the title in 1807, and married in 1825 the daugther of Archbishop Vernon of York, becoming brother-in-law to William Vernon (Harcourt). He was M.P. for Scarborough.

Hackness village, according to Whellan's *History and Topography of the City of York and The North Riding of Yorkshire* (1859), was 'delightfully situated in a romantic vale, 6 miles N.W. by W. of Scarbro'. The hills that surround the vale are from 100 to 120 yards in perpendicular height, and their steep acclivities are profusely adorned with lofty trees of the richest foliage. The road from Scarbro' to Hackness lies over Hare Brow, a lofty eminence, from which is a noble prospect of Scarborough Castle, the coast, the ocean, and the surrounding country. The descent from this hill to the beautiful vale of Hackness lies along a precipitous edge of a glen, the sides of which are adorned with lofty trees.' Part of this description is drawn from Samuel Lewis's *Topographical Dictionary of England* (1832), which continues, ' Springs of water, rushing in natural cascades from the sides of the hills, or falling with gentle murmurs, contribute to the beauty of the scenery; and the Derwent, which has its source in the mountainous country to the north, glides in a gentle stream past the village.'

In the 1830s Hackness parish had a population of about 630, with 143 living in the village itself. Hackness Hall, according to Whellan, 'a fine mansion in a most picturesque situation; with beautiful pleasure grounds planned with exquisite taste', was built by Sir Richard Johnstone.

6 Scarborough Museum was opened in 1830, as Whellan's *History and Topography of the City of York and the North Riding of Yorkshire* describes:

This chaste and elegant cut stone structure, which is situated on the northern side of the Cliff Bridge, was originated by the Scarborough Philosophical Society, in consequence of the munificent offer of the late Thomas Duesbery, Esq., of Beverley, to give the splendid collection of fossil remains, minerals, and other specimens of natural history and antiquity, formed by his uncle, Thomas Hinderwell, Esq., the late venerable historian of Scarborough, on condition that a suitable building should be raised, in which to place it. A subscription was immediately set on foot by the members of the Philosophical Society, and the foundation stone of the Museum was laid by Sir J.V.B. Johnstone, Bart., the President on the 9th of April, 1828. The cost of the building, including the purchase of ground, fitting up, etc., was £1,836 (the cost of the building alone being about £1,300) and the Museum was opened for the purpose of lectures, etc., on the 13th of February, 1830.

The edifice is a rotunda, with a dome, of the Roman Doric Order, 37½ feet in its external diameter, and 50 feet high. The circular plan of the building was suggested by W. Smith, LLD., the celebrated geologist, as being more capable of exhibiting, in one simple and intelligible form, the stratification of the rocks of Great Britain, then could be obtained by any other method . . . The classical design of the building is from the pencil of R.H. Sharpe, Esq., architect, of York. The basement contains the library, laboratory, and keeper's room, and the principal room, which is 35 feet high, is reached by a spiral staircase . . .

On ascending the staircase, the first objects which attract the eye are the fossil remains of former ages, which are placed on sloping shelves around the Museum, corresponding in some degree with the arrangement of the strata, or their natural position within the earth . . . on the first shelf are placed, as being the most recent formations, the bones which have been recovered from the remarkable Cave of Kirkdale, in Yorkshire . . . the next shelf contains the fossils from the Suffolk Crag and Paris Clay, the most recent *stratified* formations - the next, those from the Chalk; and so on, in succession, beginning with those fossils, which have been collected from the strata *most recently* formed in the crust of the globe, and proceeding the the *lower*, and *lower* beds, until we come to the primitive or granitic rocks, in which no remains of living animals can be found.

7 Rev. Adam Sedgwick, F.R.S. (1785-1873) - Educated at Trinity College, Cambridge. Made a fellow in 1810, and Woodwardian Professor of Geology 1818-73. President of the Geological Society, 1831, and awarded the Wollaston Medal in 1851. Member of a Royal Commission into the state of Cambridge University 1850-52. President of the British Association, 1833, when the annual meeting was at Cambridge, and President of the Geological Section 1837, 1845, 1853, and 1860. Prebendary of Norwich, 1834. Published papers on geology and other subjects, and helped to expand the University's collection of geological specimens.

William Henry Wollaston (1766-1828) - Educated at Charterhouse and Caius College, Cambridge, training as a phsyician. He was a senior fellow of Caius, 1787-1828, and practised at Huntingdon and Bury St. Edmunds before moving to London in 1797. He retired from medicine in 1800 and engaged in chemical research; he devised a method of producing pure platinum and of welding it to make vessels, and published papers on many subjects, including medicine, mineralogy, astromony, and the study of electricity. Secretary to the Royal Society, 1804-16. On his death in 1828, he left bequests to the Royal Society and to the Geological Society, the latter forming the 'Wollaston Fund'.

The Wollaston Medal was awarded to William Smith, in the words of its citation:

In consideration of his being a great original discoverer in English geology; and especially for his being the first in this country to discover and to teach the identification of strata, and to determine their succession by means of their imbedded fossils.

*   *   *